Emotional Buoyancy

Kiley Albrecht

Presentation by *BookLeaf Publishing*

Web: www.bookleafpub.com

E-mail: info@bookleafpub.com

ISBN: 9789358369021

First edition 2024

PREFACE

Inspired by the likes of Abraham Hicks and Dr. David R. Hawkins, this book of poems spans the scale of human emotions. When we find ourselves in the low vibration of shame, it's all but impossible to jump straight to joy. The two emotions are simply too vibrationally far away from each other. However, from shame we can more easily access sadness, and from there move up toward happiness and beyond. Whether you read this book from start to finish, or start from the emotion you currently feel, my sincere intent is for you to float your way as high as you'll allow yourself to go.

Shame

Hand by careful hand, I've built my disguise.
But my best poker face doesn't conceal
the royal flush beneath my skin.

I'm the queen of heart-drops.

Card by nervous card, I construct a refuge,
trying to finish before anyone notices I'm here.

The queen of hearts drops.

As it tumbles to the floor,
I feel everyone's snake eyes on me.

All I can think is are there really no better places
to look than my attempt to exist correctly
enough to avoid a collapsing house of cards?

Guilt

It's been said there's a pearl in the center of the ocean, and that finding it would be the highest accomplishment of the world.

Dusk falls as he looks out at the horizon through a pearl-sized hole in his heart.

How could he ever take on the ocean, who humbly bestows all life when all he can do is find fault with the sunset?

Yet with time, the hole and the pearl lure him into the water.

Sinking down, he can no longer tell the sinking of his heart.

"Thank goodness," he thinks, as legend says he can only claim the pearl if he manages not to cry. "Then again, could the ocean really tell my tears?"

Drifting among the plankton, he doesn't care to meet their gaze. The seaweed waves a greeting, but he's too busy scoffing under his breath at the coral reef: "Stupid overachievers of the ocean."

He swims aimlessly until he's almost too tired to move, barely managing to grab hold of a passing tailfin the size of his self-reproach.

When his tears threaten to speak up for his center, he reminds them of the glory of the pearl. The pearl made by the ocean who bestows all life--his own life, and that of the tail he holds in a grip he fears won't ever let go.

The water pushes past his face as he closes his eyes.

Indeed, the ocean does know his tears, even before he does.

They mix with the waters and change the current just enough to loosen his hand.

As if summoned, coming into focus right in front of him, there it is.

The little white shining sphere of glory that promises so much.

It's so close.

So close he could have reached out and touched it.

Despair

On city streets so far from home,
a wicked symphony plays on a loop.

Listlessly, I urge each of my legs to leave
and find the ground again.

It seems the passing trucks don't care
how loud they are,
or that they don't have to find their own way
like I do.

I can tell it's supposed to smell like wet
pavement and roasted street cashews,
but someone's Marlboro lungs are practicing
poor boundaries again.

I turn the corner enough times to realize all turns
lead to the same anonymous place.
The same poisonous air,
the same fortissimo of drive-by sirens,
the same crescendo of semi-truck compression
brakes.

Sadness

I woke up and can't seem to find my glasses
or my happiness anywhere.
I looked in the places I left them last night,
but they aren't there.

I can see that the rooms and objects
look the same as before,
but something in them is missing.
I think it's the same thing that's missing
from a movie set replica of a familiar place.
But more heart-wrenching.

In this version of the world, gravity somehow
pulls stronger on just my heart.
And solace comes from nowhere
save for bathroom stalls, shower walls,
and my pillow after night falls.

Fear

Phone slowly placed face up across the table,
his finger over the call button, eerily unstable.

My stomach turns upside down,
making me wanna run,
when I make out the numbers
on the screen: 9-1-1.

His eyes tell me to act normal
despite the circumstances,
that knives can be tucked away
in jackets, socks, and certain glances.

I look down at my plate, hoping
his fears are unfounded.
But he's noticed what I'm about to--
that we're causally surrounded.

In a cold sweat I realize the guy at the payphone
never put in a quarter.
And the one in the booth behind us
never put in an order.

Craving

Parties don't worry you.
Danger doesn't hurry you.
You're access to excess,
a lack of what connects us.

That pit in my solar plexus.

So I people please
in hopes of guarantees,
thinking impossible perfection
could prevent possible rejection.

How nice must it be,
to be free to that degree,
to never have the feeling,
"What about me?"

Rage

The storm in my chest moves into my head,
is about to come out of my mouth,
but I siphon it down and let it mix
with the acid in my stomach.

Charged air and my vitriolic stare
give the room a poisonous potential.

How conventional.

I'm ready to start a sonic fire,
with jagged-edged phrases
and distorted logic mazes.

But I know better.

Words won't make a point quite like the echoes,
of silence and walking away in stilettos.

Anger

Pounded tables
and scapegoat convictions.
Slammed drawers
and vasoconstrictions.

Hijacked bodies react
in sheep's clothing.
Electrified egos project
their self-loathing.

Poor connections,
muted by hindered hearts,
as the goats and the sheep
keep playing their parts.

Pride

I am such a genius
(I flip my golden hair).
I know, it's gorgeous,
but don't be creepy when you stare.

I could never do brunette,
or settle for silver or bronze.
For me it's golden hour all the time,
not just dusks and dawns.

Anyway, I'm bored, can you move?
I'm trying to take a selfie.
No, I'm not a gold digger,
but yes, of course he's wealthy.

You know, it's really not my fault
I'm in such high demand,
or that he's wrapped around my finger
like a 12 carat wedding band.

I can't help I'm such a precious gem,
a treasure to behold,
or that everything I talk about
just so happens to be gold.

Worry

Stomach tightens, breathing quickens.
Opposing forces draw their weapons.
The sympathetic nervous system
isn't very sympathetic, is it?
Heart rate.
Heart, wait.

Time keeps these secrets, for now.
But Time always tells secrets, somehow.

Pacing.
Ok, be mindful.
Mind full?
Mine's full.

I'm sinking in a sea of questions,
a tea of suggestions.

If all likelihoods compete,
what if the wrong ones retreat?

Doubt

What to think in a world where thoughts are free but feelings come at a cost? Or do our thoughts cost a penny?

Either way, I better have a lot of pennies because the person directing all this stop-and-go mind traffic definitely takes a toll.

Granted, it is a skill to know which thought has the right of way and which way has the right of thought.

I don't think I'd know how to evaluate all the factors and potential causes. There would also be the conditions and permutations to take into account, as well as all the reasons and exceptions. But what if I missed one, or forgot to check the inverses? I suppose the converses would also need to be considered, but at the same time, truth is subjective, so in the end might it not all be moot?

Is there maybe someone we could talk to?

Excuse me, Ms. Intellectual-Traffic Worker,

What's the protocol for runaway thought trucks
if the escape ramp is under construction?

Irritation

Lemme call you right back, Disappointment's at
the door and I have to show him the
"Appointments Only" sign again.

He tends to miss things like that since his eyes
are always cast down to keep from tripping over
his dignity.

I told him to keep it in a tin can or something so
he can hear it when it drops, but he probably
couldn't hear me over the sound of his dragging
feet.

When I ask him to leave, he mutters something
about "expectations."

My facial arrangement tells him that with so
many deadlines and requirements to meet, what
makes him think I have time for expectations?

Courage

Step one: Two feet on the ground.
Okay, standing upright.

Now, how on earth to proceed
without it being a fight?

Well, the same way a redwood gets
three hundred feet high,
and the rivers find
oceans without having to try.

The same way the squirrel leaps
to far, flimsy branches,
and the starlings in formation do
their dazzling dances.

The same way a caterpillar knows
exactly what to do,
watch what happens when you realize
you do too.

Contentment

"Sweetheart, you don't have to hide anymore."
She says it with so much certainty, he knows it
must be true.

As his glistening gaze meets hers, the old pink
ribbon and barbed wire fall to the floor.
His chest feels unfamiliar.

He slowly takes a sip of tea and thinks.
Why didn't I know this before?

The scent of jasmine flowers floats in with the
sun to remind him of a couple things that soften
his shoulders, and his heart.

Suddenly, breathing's never made so much
sense. He comments, "That which comes in on
the wind doesn't threaten much, does it?"

She replies, "Oh darling, don't you know?
There is no threat. There is no threat."

Optimism

A flower may wrinkle,
and wither, and fall.
But look closely, a flower
is much like it all.
Just as it seems
to be here and then gone,
so does the sun, moon,
and Tuesday at dawn.

What's wrong becomes right,
and what's dark becomes light.
Ride the waves of illusion,
but don't hold too tight.

While Frost may say
nothing gold can stay,
rest assured, new gold comes
with every new day.

Belief

I listen as truth warns how much is at stake,
yet leaves a small glimmer of hope in its wake.

I follow it down,
all the way to the horizon--
Labyrinthine. Unseen.
Like a dream.

Through invisible mirrors,
I see as I did during my first days on Earth.

My breath mixes me with the atmosphere
as the wind brings me a long-lost memory:

Hydrogen bred and supernova born,
I can make my own fate.
I'm all I ever needed,
I'm starlight incarnate.

Understanding

I was so deep in rumination I didn't even realize
the set-up.

One domino to the next
as if in some determined hurry
to reach
the other side.
Did the winding
row stop at the end of
the table,
or continue underneath?

I could have sworn I saw the last standing piece
smirk at physics as it fell.
Maybe I confused its fear for defiance.
Or its dots for dimples.

If only the little black and white soldiers lined
the Earth and not the table,
the question of winding underneath wouldn't be
so relevant.

My humble rectangular soldiers,
if you so wish to progress,
stand back up, straight and still.

At attention.
Pay attention.
And I assure you it will pay you back.
You'll understand better
how things can flow both ways.

Like circles.
Circles are unrelenting.
Circles are predictable.
Ruminations are my little circles.

I wonder how I feel about triangles.
Yes, maybe I'll try angles.
Angles create a more accurate picture
of the whole.

Though circles are whole too.
Or are they holes?
Either way, I'd like to circle back to angles,
but the arm of my clock is headstrong.
Or is it handstrong?

Pardon me, please pause.

Would you mind being patient with me while I
organize my mind into a neat stack of neurology
so that the misplaced thoughts may line up with
the breathing of the universe?
…

Okay, everything's in its place,
and it's come to my attention
that the missing piece all along
was a lack of dimension.

Enthusiasm

I leap with a free heart
and iridescent thoughts.
The yum of it all makes me want
to scream in Solfeggio tones.

Graceful as a ballerina butterfly
carried by her rainbow laugh,
all of nature goes along
with my celestial dance.

Celebratory and light.
Defying gravity.
I rise up up up,
through velvet clouds,
above everything.

In the rapturous emptiness,
I see only a single Ruppell's Griffon Vulture.

Of course I say yes when it wants to tell me
the secrets of the universe,
and laugh with joy when I know
I don't understand.

Love

She walked past him by the coffee shop
on Los Feliz Blvd,
as if the street name knew their destiny.

He didn't ask for a glance, or a chance,
but then again neither did she.
The moment he smiled to himself
was the moment she somehow
was already walking beside him,
as if she always had been.

The sound of her kitten heels
on the pavement spoke first,
but his playful saunter carried the convo.

Each step became part
of the music of their world,
building carefully to the chorus
that took them to the bridge.

Starlight and laughter led them across it,
and forever and ever the melody
never sounded so good.

Joy

Have you ever noticed the heart
doesn't see the illusions of the senses?

It sees in timeless holograms,
in blinking flecks of possibility.

Each one contains the whole
universe, you know.
In outer space, and inner, there is no
up or down or back or forth.
So naturally, nothing and everything
must be right.

If you let yourself, you can hear
the quantum whispers of reassurance,
and feel the electromagnetic pulses
of ultimate relief.

Have you ever noticed it's not just
the mouth that can smile?

Peace

Come with me.

Let's brew potentiali-tea as dystopia collapses
under the weightlessness of harmony.

Look on as Abundance shows Beg, Borrow,
and Steal a smile as big as the world.

The only words we find are made of honey.
The only questions we have make solutions.

And when silence comes,
it feels like everything we've ever wanted.

Now we know who we are.
We are you, and we are me, don't you see?

We're free.